SATs Practice
MATHS

FOR AGES 9–10

Introduction

The government's optional tests for Year 5 pupils consist of a mental maths test and two written papers (calculator and non-calculator). Because the same optional tests are re-issued every year there are no past papers on which children can practise so this book provides four practice papers as an alternative. If you would also like to give the children experience of the mental maths test then *Mental Maths Tests for Ages 9-10 Andrew Brodie*, provides excellent practice for this.

This book contains four test papers, two for pupils to complete without a calculator and two with a calculator and an answer sections for each paper. The tests reflect the style and content of the optional tests for Year 5 and are designed to familiarise children and teachers with the format of these tests. Each test is slightly shorter than the actual optional test for Year 5. In the tests in this book the pupils are allowed 35 minutes to complete each test, rather than the 45 minutes in the optional tests.

To make the tests as realistic as possible, each one can be made into a booklet and so the pages are numbered from 1 to 16 for each test. To make up the booklet you need to lay them out in such a way that you can photocopy them on to A3 paper, back to back. If you decide to do this you will need four sheets of A3 paper to make a 16-page booklet and to photocopy them in the following way:

Pages 1 and 16 backed with pages 2 and 15
Pages 3 and 14 backed with pages 4 and 13
Pages 5 and 12 backed with pages 6 and 11
Pages 7 and 10 backed with pages 8 and 9

Each test contains 22 questions, matched appropriately to National Curriculum Programmes of Study (see the Contents page for each test). You may decide to concentrate on one page at a time with your pupils, discussing each question in detail and using it as a teaching opportunity as well as practice in how pupils should write the answers.

At the end of the book is a Class record sheet which can be used to record individual pupils' marks for each question. When used in conjunction with the Contents page, this is very useful for analysing the class' performance as it can reveal gaps in skills or knowledge. Any such 'gaps' can then be addressed in maths lessons before your pupils sit the 'real' test in Year 6.

Making a judgement about the level that each child has achieved

In the National tests a level is allocated based on the pupil's score in Test A, Test B and the Mental Maths Test. In this book we provide a system for finding an approximate level, without using the Mental Maths Test score.

Tests A1 and A2 are both non-calculator papers and tests B1 and B2 are both calculator papers. To gain an indication of an individual pupil's performance, add together her/his score from an A test and from a B test. The total score available for the two tests is 50 marks.

Use the chart below to get an indication of the pupil's level of achievement.

Pupil's score	Possible National Curriculum Level
0 – 10	below level 3
11 – 16	level 3C
17 – 22	level 3B
23 – 27	level 3A
28 – 33	level 4C
34 – 38	level 4B
39 – 42	level 4A
43 – 46	level 5C
47 – 50	level 5B

Contents of Test A1 (non-calculator)

Key stage 2, Year 5
Mathematics practice booklet
Test A1

Name

Score

Level and grade

Do **not** use a calculator for any questions in this test.

Levels 3–5

Do **not** use a calculator when working on this test.

Work quickly but carefully.

Your teacher will time the test – you will be allowed 35 minutes.

If you find a question very difficult, miss it out and move on to the next question. You will be able to return to the question later if you have time.

If you finish all the questions before the end of the 35 minutes it's a good idea to go back and check your work.

Write your answers in the answer boxes. If you need to do any working out you can use anywhere else on the page.

If the question says 'show your working' you must do so – you **may** get an extra mark.

1 Calculate

769 + 83

Q1
1 mark

---

2 Eggs are packed in boxes of 6.

There are 70 eggs.

How many boxes can be filled?

Q2i
1 mark

How many eggs are left over?

Q2ii
1 mark

Total

3 Look at the numbers.

Tick the multiples of 5.

14   15   16   17   18

19   20   21   22   23

24   25   26

4 Look at these numbers.

$2\frac{1}{2}$ $1\frac{1}{4}$ $\frac{1}{2}$ $2\frac{1}{4}$ $1\frac{3}{4}$ $2\frac{3}{4}$

Write the numbers in the correct places.

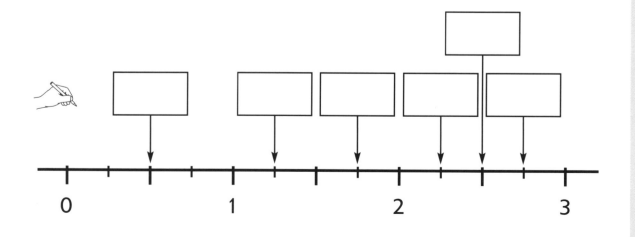

5 Sanjeev is 126cm tall.

Write Sanjeev's height in metres.

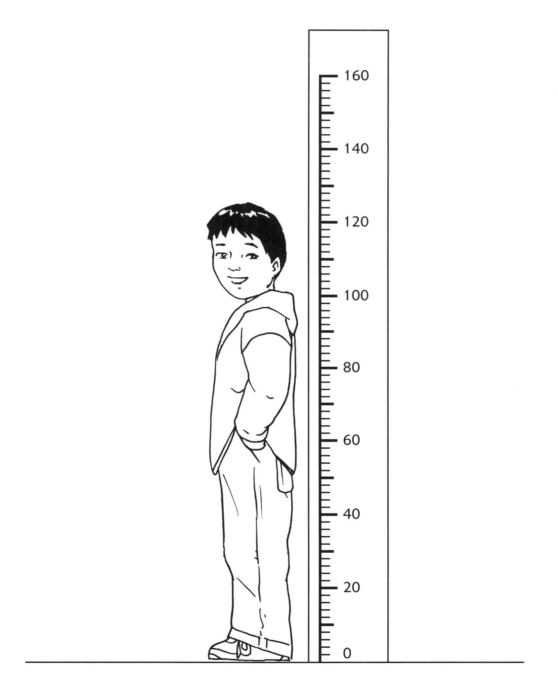

Q5
1 mark

Total

6 Write this set of numbers in order, starting with the smallest.

649   946   694   496   964   469

Q6
1 mark

7 Round this number to the nearest whole number.

to the nearest whole number

3.6 ⟶

Q7
1 mark

Total

8

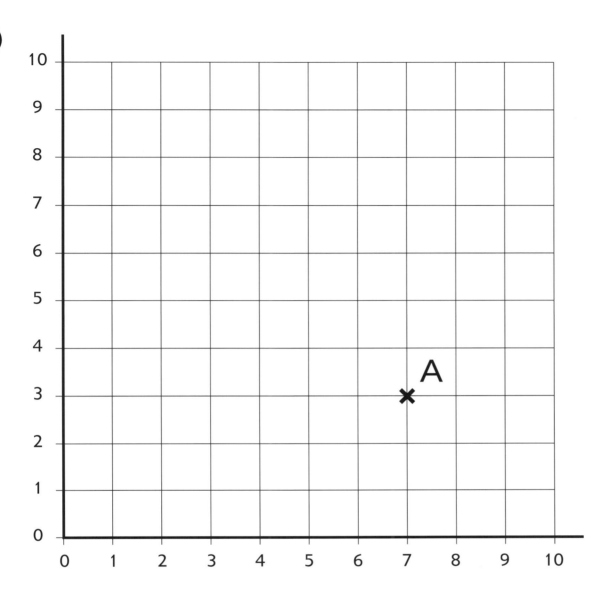

Write the coordinates of the point marked A.

Q8
1 mark

---

9 What number is double 95?

Q9
1 mark

Total

10 Here are two additions that make 16:

$$12 + 4 = 16$$

$$10 + 6 = 16$$

Write five more additions of whole numbers to make 16.

$\boxed{} + \boxed{} = 16$

$\boxed{} + \boxed{} = 16$

$\boxed{} + \boxed{} = 16$

$\boxed{} + \boxed{} = 16$

$\boxed{} + \boxed{} = 16$

Q10
1 mark

Total

11 Jess wants to buy four oranges.

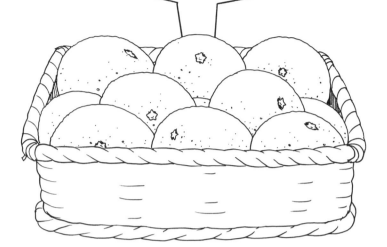

Oranges
42ᵖ each

How much will she have to pay?

Q11i
1 mark

How much change will she have from £2?

Q11ii
1 mark

Total

12

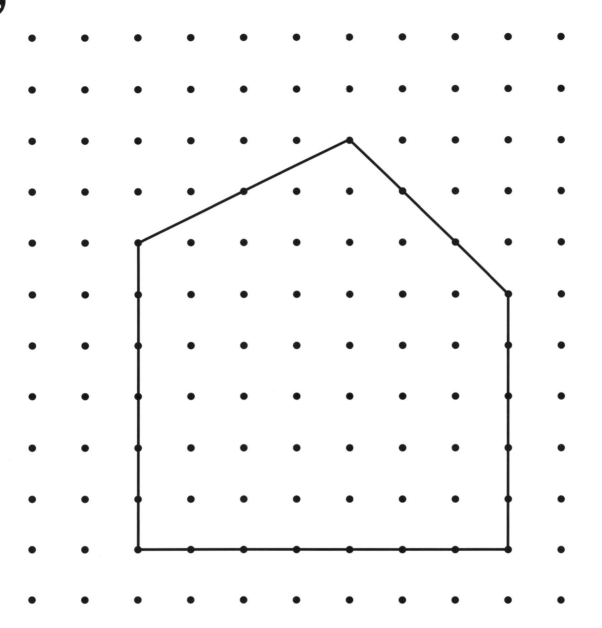

What is the name of this shape?

Mark the two right angles on the shape.

Andrew Brodie: SATs Practice Maths for ages 9–10   10   © A&C Black Publishers Ltd 2007   14   **Test A1**

Q12i
1 mark

Q12ii
1 mark

Total

13 Convert 1 litre to millilitres.

$$1 \text{ litre} = \boxed{} \text{ millilitres}$$

Q13
1 mark

14 Look at this rectangle.

Measure it accurately to find its perimeter.

Q14
1 mark

Total

15 Sanjeev's bedroom clock shows this time.

This is his kitchen clock.

Draw the hands on the clock so that it shows the same time as the bedroom clock.

Q15
1 mark

Total

16 The graph shows the temperature at noon on each school day for a week.

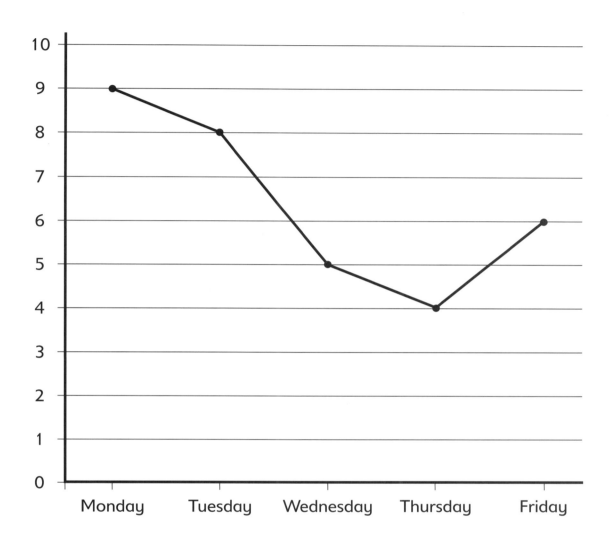

On which day was the temperature lowest?

Q16i
1 mark

What is the range of the temperatures?

Q16ii
1 mark

Total

17 Write the next number in the sequence.

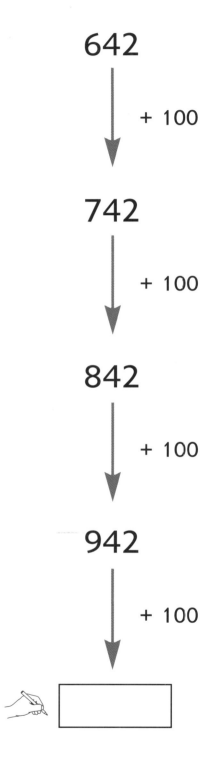

Q17
1 mark

Total

18 Draw a ring around each prime number.

One is done for you.

9

12

10

(11)

19

20

15

16

13

14

18

17

Q18
1 mark

---

19 Calculate

46 × 10

---

20 What number is half of 48?

Q20
1 mark

21 Draw all the lines of symmetry on these shapes.

Q21i
1 mark

Q21ii
1 mark

Total

Answers to Test A1 (non-calculator)

When marking the children's work it is suggested that you enter marks in the boxes provided in the margins:

Enter 1 for a correct answer.

Enter 0 for an incorrect answer.

Enter – for no answer written.

Question	Answer	Mark	Notes
1	852	1	
2i	11	1	Check that pupils realise that the boxes must be full.
2ii	4	1	
3	15, 20, 25	1	Take the opportunity to remind pupils that multiples of 5 always end with 5 or 0.
4	✓ correct number line	1	
5	1.26m	1	Ensure pupils write m for metre.
6	469, 496, 649, 694, 946, 964	1	
7	4	1	
8	(7, 3)	1	Ensure pupils write 7 first.
9	190	1	
10	Accept all appropriate	1	
11i	£1.68 or 168p	1	
11ii	32p or £0.32	1	Common mistake is 42p.
12i	Pentagon	1	

Question	Answer	Mark	Notes
12ii	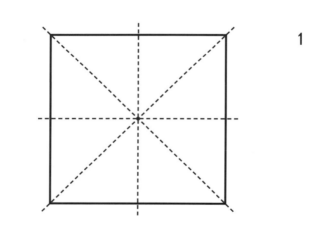	1	
13	1000 millilitres	1	
14	26cm	1	
15	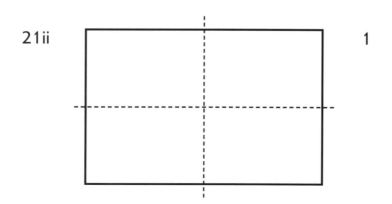	1	Ensure that the hour hand is correctly positioned a quarter of the way between 11 and 12.
16i	Thursday	1	
16ii	5°C	1	
17	1042	1	
18	11, 13, 17, 19	1	
19	460	1	
20	24	1	

21i

1

21ii

1

Contents of Test A2 (non-calculator)

Key stage 2, Year 5
Mathematics practice booklet
Test A2

Name

Score

Level and grade

Do not use a calculator for any questions in this test.

Levels 3–5

Do **not** use a calculator when working on this test.

Work quickly but carefully.

Your teacher will time the test – you will be allowed 35 minutes.

If you find a question very difficult, miss it out and move on to the next question. You will be able to return to the question later if you have time.

If you finish all the questions before the end of the 35 minutes it's a good idea to go back and check your work.

Write your answers in the answer boxes. If you need to do any working out you can use anywhere else on the page.

If the question says 'show your working' you must do so – you **may** get an extra mark.

1 Calculate

$$614 - 89$$

Q1
1 mark

2 Calculate

$$265 + 159$$

Q2
1 mark

3 What is the total number of hours in 3 days?

Show your working – you may get an extra mark.

Q3i
1 mark

Q3ii
1 mark

Total

4 Look at this boat viewed from above.

It is pointing towards the north.

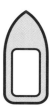

It turns 90° clockwise.

One of the pictures below shows it now.

 Put a tick by the correct picture.

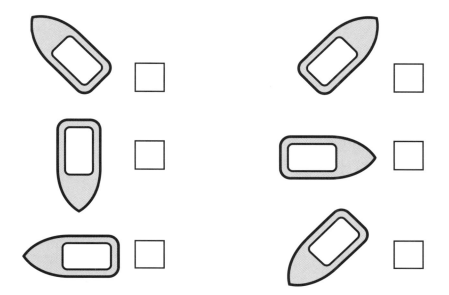

Q4i
1 mark

In which direction is the boat pointing now?

 Put a tick by the correct answer.

North ☐   South ☐   South-West ☐

West ☐   South-East ☐   East ☐

North-East ☐   North-West ☐

Q4ii
1 mark

Total

5 What volume of water is in the measuring cylinder?

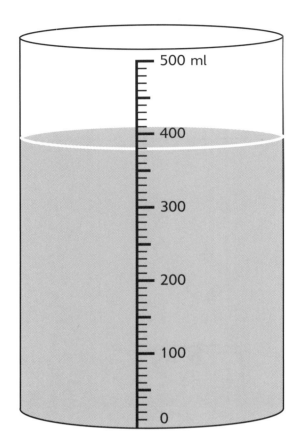

Q5
1 mark

---

6 This is the timetable for a school hall one morning.

| 9 am | | 10 am | 10.30 am | 10.45 am | | 12 noon |

| CLASS 4 | ASSEMBLY | BREAK | CLASS 3 |

How many minutes longer does Class 3 have than Class 4?

Q6
1 mark

Total

7 Show the next number in this sequence.

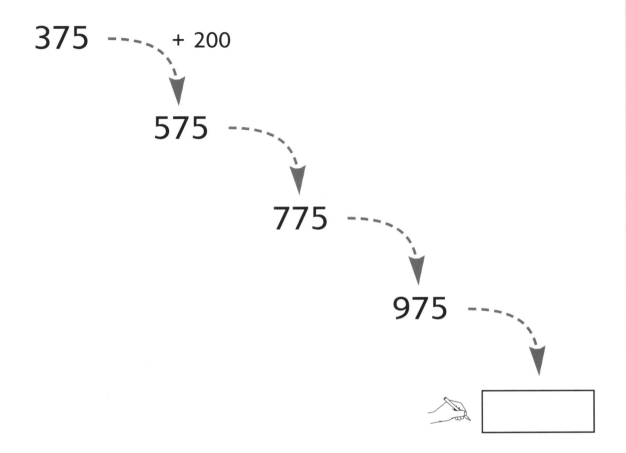

375 ----→ + 200

575

775

975

---

8 Look at these symbols: <   >   =

Write the correct symbol in each box.

2 × 10 [   ] 36 ÷ 2

$\frac{1}{2}$ of 100 [   ] 2 × 25

9 Here is a calendar page showing July.

July

Monday	Tuesday	Wednesday	Thursday	Friday	Saturday	Sunday
1	2	3	4	5	6	7
8	9	10	11	12	13	14
15	16	17	18	19	20	21
22	23	24	25	26	27	28
29	30	31				

On what day of the week is 3rd August?

Q9i
1 mark

On what day of the week is 30th June?

Q9ii
1 mark

Total

10 The lines show two sides of an irregular hexagon.

Draw more lines to complete the hexagon.

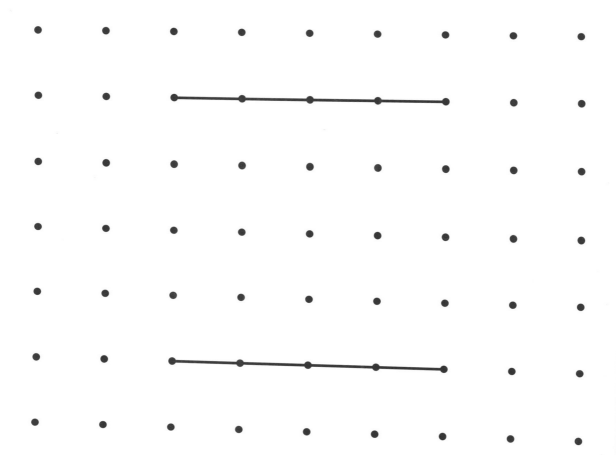

Q10
1 mark

11 Tick the shape that is **not** the net of a cube.

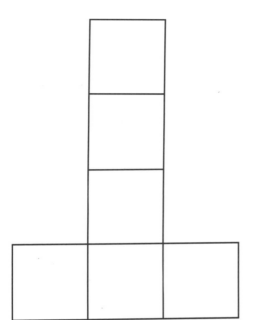

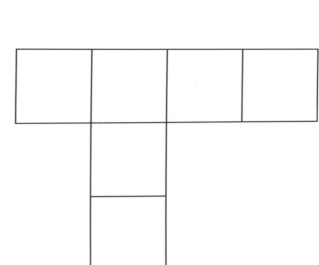

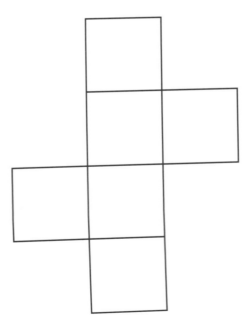

Q11
1 mark

Total

Test A2

12 Write the correct number in the box.

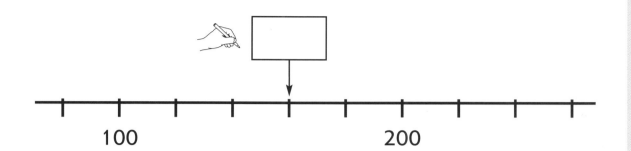

100   200

Q12
1 mark

---

13 Tick the two divisions that have a remainder of 3.

$$18 \div 5$$

$$19 \div 3$$

$$27 \div 4$$

$$14 \div 6$$

Q13
1 mark

Total

14 What temperature is shown on the thermometer?

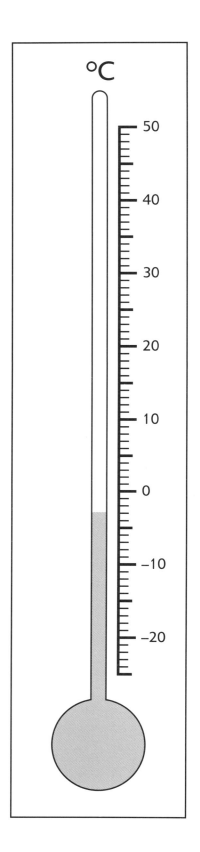

Q14
1 mark

Total

15 Here are three digit cards.

| 3 | | 2 | | 4 |

Use the cards to make the numbers on the number line.

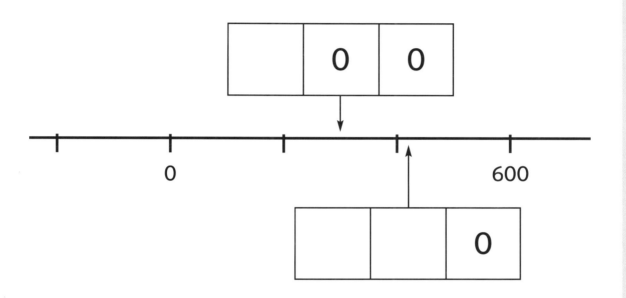

| | 0 | 0 |

0   600

| | | 0 |

Q15
1 mark

---

16 Calculate

$$4169 + 3854$$

Q16
1 mark

Total

17 Measure angle S accurately, using a protractor or angle measurer.

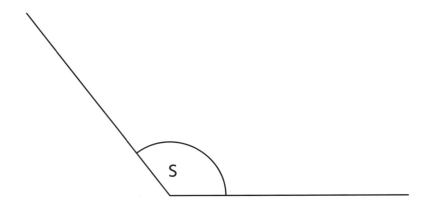

Q17
1 mark

---

18 Calculate

$$8 - 1.7$$

Q18
1 mark

Total

19 Postman Pete counted the number of letters delivered to each house in a street.

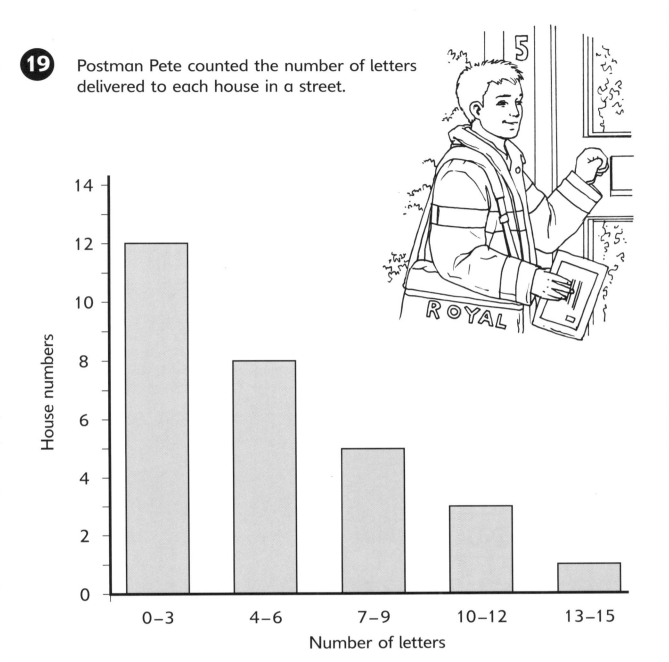

How many houses received fewer than 7 letters?

20 Write these numbers in order.

One has been done for you.

| 1.6 | 6.1 | 1.06 |
| 6.01 | 1.66 | 6.66 |

smallest

[ ]

1.6

[ ]

[ ]

[ ]

[ ]

largest

Q20
1 mark

Total

21 Calculate

$$861 \div 7$$

Q21
1 mark

---

22 Calculate

$$6000 - 1416$$

Q22
1 mark

Total

Answers to Test A2 (non-calculator)

When marking the children's work it is suggested that you enter marks in the boxes provided in the margins:

Enter 1 for a correct answer.

Enter 0 for an incorrect answer.

Enter – for no answer written.

Question	Answer	Mark	Notes
1	525	1	
2	424	1	
3i	72	1	
3ii	Appropriate calculations	1	
4i		1	
4ii	East	1	
5	380ml	1	Encourage pupils to observe closely the calibration of the measuring cylinder.
6	15 minutes	1	
7	1175	1	
8i	>	1	
8ii	=	1	
9i	Saturday	1	Encourage pupils to read the question carefully.
9ii	Sunday	1	
10		1	Accept any hexagon – the number of sides must, of course, be six.

Question	Answer	Mark	Notes
11	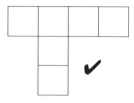	1	
12	160	1	Encourage pupils to observe the value of each marker.
13	18 ÷ 5 27 ÷ 4	1	
14	-3°C	1	Ensure pupils observe the negative values on the thermometer.
15	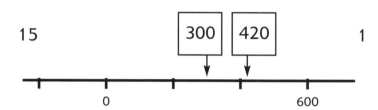	1	
16	8023	1	Ensure pupils calculate neatly as they are less likely to make mistakes.
17	127°	1	Ensure pupils read from the correct zero marker on the protractor.
18	6.3	1	
19	20	1	Ensure pupils understand 'fewer'.
20	1.06, 1.6, 1.66, 6.01, 6.1, 6.66	1	
21	123	1	
22	4584	1	

Contents of Test B1 (calculator)

Key stage 2, Year 5

Mathematics practice booklet

Test B1

Name

Score

Level and grade

You may use a calculator for any questions in this test.

Levels 3–5

Instructions

You **may** use a calculator when working on this test. You will not need a calculator for every question.

Work quickly but carefully.

Your teacher will time the test – you will be allowed 35 minutes.

If you find a question very difficult, miss it out and move on to the next question. You will be able to return to the question later if you have time.

If you finish all the questions before the end of the 35 minutes it's a good idea to go back and check your work.

Write your answers in the answer boxes. If you need to do any working out you can use anywhere else on the page.

If the question says 'show your working' you must do so – you **may** get an extra mark.

1 The number in each square is equal to the sum of the numbers in the circles on either side.

Write the missing numbers.

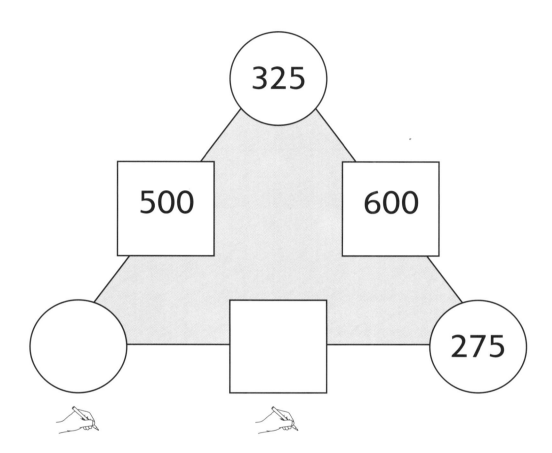

Q1
1 mark

---

2 Write the next number in the sequence.

Q2
1 mark

Total

---

3 Write the missing number in the box.

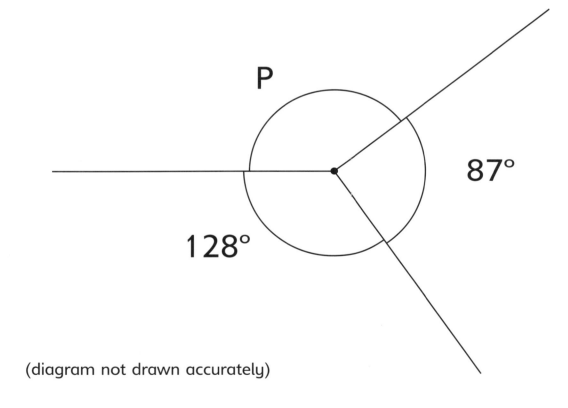

$\boxed{} \times 36 = 288$

Q3
1 mark

4 Calculate the size of angle p.

P

87°

128°

(diagram not drawn accurately)

Q4
1 mark

Total

5 Write the missing number in the box.

$$12.5 \times 5 = \boxed{} \div 2$$

6 The shaded triangle is isosceles.

Write the coordinates of point B.

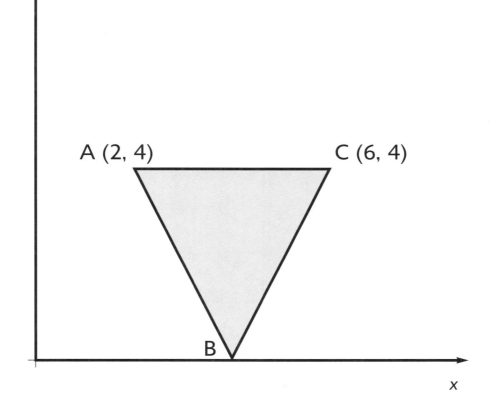

7 Draw the reflection of the shape in the mirror line.

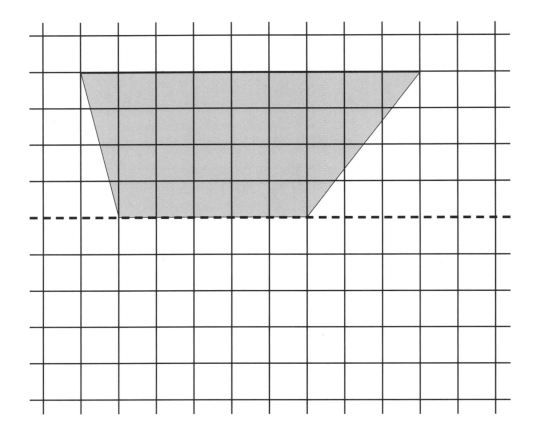

Q7
1 mark

8 Write the missing number in the box.

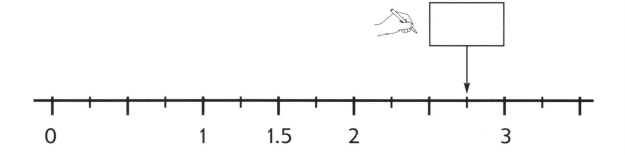

0   1   1.5   2   3

Q8
1 mark

Total

9 Four equally priced T-shirts cost £24.60 altogether.

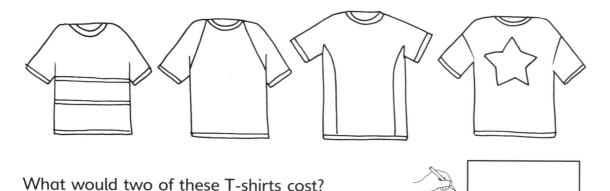

What would two of these T-shirts cost?

Q9
1 mark

10 Look at the shape.

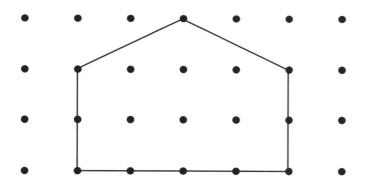

Imagine the shape is rotated 90° clockwise.

Draw the rotated shape.

Q10
1 mark

Total

11 The full bottle holds 1 litre.

Q11
1 mark

Jess pours out 476ml.

How much is left in the bottle?

Total

12 A farmer uses fences to make a sheep pen that is 12 metres long and 4 metres wide.

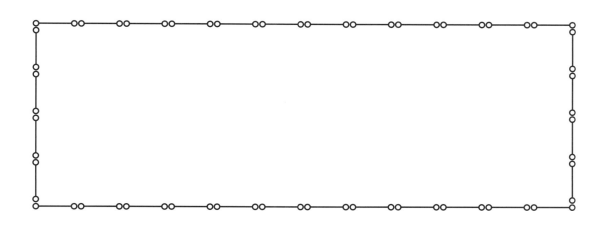

What is the perimeter of the sheep pen?

Q12i
1 mark

He changes his mind and decides to use exactly the same fences to make a square pen.

What will be the length of each side?

Q12ii
1 mark

Total

13 Calculate

$$\frac{1}{6} \text{ of } 222$$

Q13
1 mark

14 100 children come to the school hall for dinner.

8 children can fit at each dinner table.

How many tables are needed for all of them to sit down at the same time?

Show your working. You may get an extra mark.

Q14i
1 mark

Q14ii
1 mark

Total

15 Match each shape to its name.

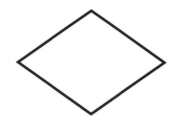

trapezium

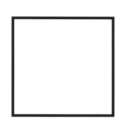

parallelogram

square

rhombus

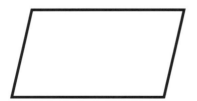

rectangle

Q15
1 mark

Total

16 Three caravans are for sale.

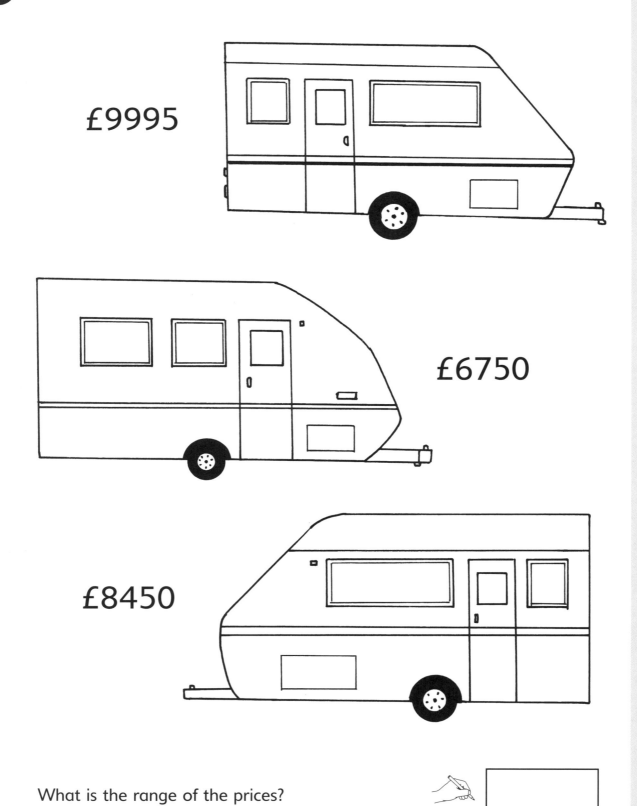

£9995

£6750

£8450

What is the range of the prices?

Q16
1 mark

12 54 **Test B1**

Total

17 Dan's class counted vehicles passing the school gate.

Here are the results.

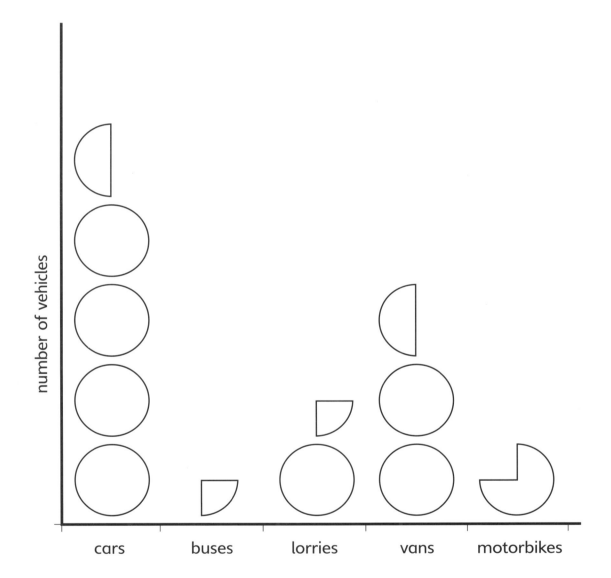

How many more vans were there than lorries?

Q17
1 mark

Total

18 Jess rolls a numbered dice.

She could get a 1, 2, 3, 4, 5 or 6.

What is her chance of rolling the numbers described in the boxes below?

Match each box to the correct word.

One has been done for you.

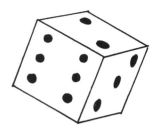

more than 1		certain
7		equally likely
an even number		likely
a number less than 8		impossible

Q18
1 mark

Total

19 Dan put a cake in the oven at this time.

10:45

It takes 25 minutes for the cake to cook.

Tick the time that the cake should come out of the oven.

10:10

10:20

11:10

11:20

11:05

10:05

Q19
1 mark

Total

20 Look at these symbols.

Write the correct symbol in the box.

 4.6×10 ☐ $50 - 5$

Q20
1 mark

---

21 Draw brackets to make this correct.

 $6 \times 4 + 3 = 42$

Q21
1 mark

---

22 Draw a line that is perpendicular to this line.

Q22
1 mark

Total

Answers to Test B1 (calculator)

When marking the children's work it is suggested that you enter marks in the boxes provided in the margins:

Enter 1 for a correct answer.

Enter 0 for an incorrect answer.

Enter – for no answer written.

Question	Answer	Mark	Notes
1	175, 450	1	A very difficult question!
2	1024	1	
3	8	1	
4	145°	1	
5	125	1	
6	(4, 0)	1	Encourage pupils to notice that B must be halfway between A and C in the x direction.
7		1	
8	2.75	1	
9	£12.30	1	Ensure that pupils write the answer correctly as money because their calculator display will show 12.3 not 12.30.
10		1	
11	524ml	1	Ensure that pupils write ml or millilitres.

12i	32m	1	Ensure that pupils write m or metres.
12ii	8m	1	
13	37	1	
14i	13 tables	1	12 remainder 4 is not an acceptable answer as the question says they must all sit down.
14ii	accept appropriate working	1	
15		1	

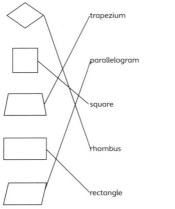

16	£3245	1	Ensure pupils understand meaning of 'range'.
17	5	1	
18		1	

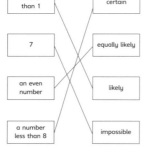

19	11.10	1	
20	>	1	
21	6 × (4 + 3) = 42	1	
22		1	

Contents of Test B2 (calculator)

Key stage 2, Year 5

Mathematics practice booklet

Test B2

Name

Score

Level and grade

Do not use a calculator for any questions in this test.

Levels 3–5

Instructions

You **may** use a calculator when working on this test. You will not need a calculator for every question.

Work quickly but carefully.

Your teacher will time the test – you will be allowed 35 minutes.

If you find a question very difficult, miss it out and move on to the next question. You will be able to return to the question later if you have time.

If you finish all the questions before the end of the 35 minutes it's a good idea to go back and check your work.

Write your answers in the answer boxes. If you need to do any working out you can use anywhere else on the page.

If the question says 'show your working' you must do so – you **may** get an extra mark.

1 Tick the two fractions that are equivalent to 0.4.

$$\frac{1}{4} \qquad \frac{4}{10} \qquad \frac{2}{5} \qquad \frac{1}{40}$$

 ☐ ☐ ☐ ☐

Q1
1 mark

2 Write the next number in this sequence.

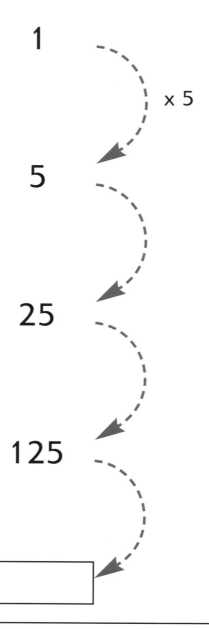

1

x 5

5

25

125

Q2
1 mark

Total

3 Draw a ring around each prime number.

25

17

18

20   22

19   16

21

24

23

Q3
1 mark

4 Draw brackets to make this calculation correct.

    4 × 12 – 2 = 40

Q4
1 mark

Total

5 Write the name of each shape in the correct
region on the Venn diagram.

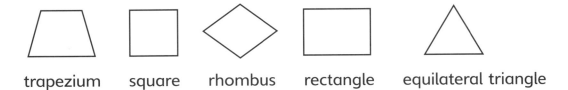

trapezium   square   rhombus   rectangle   equilateral triangle

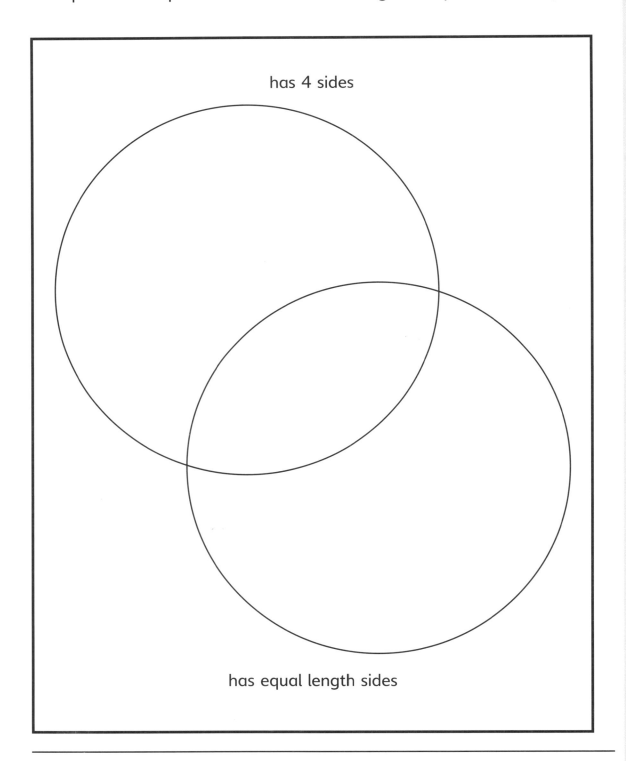

Q5
1 mark

Total

6 Calculate the size of angle y.

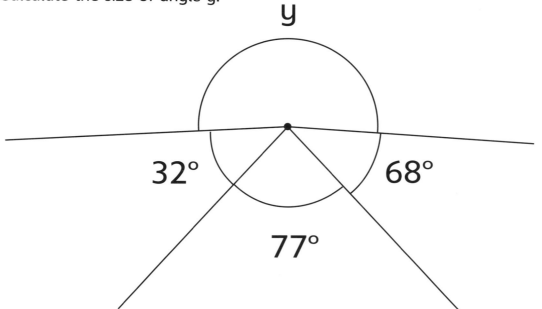

(diagram not drawn accurately)

Q6
1 mark

7 Match the measurements.

One is done for you.

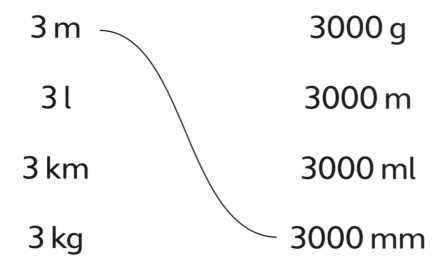

Q7
1 mark

Total

8 Calculate

$$642 \times 23$$

Q8
1 mark

9 How many hours are there in seven days?

Q9
1 mark

Total

10 The clock shows 10.50 am.

Draw hands to make this clock show the time
35 minutes later.

What time does the clock show?

Q10i
1 mark

Q10ii
1 mark

Total

11 This is a regular pentagon.

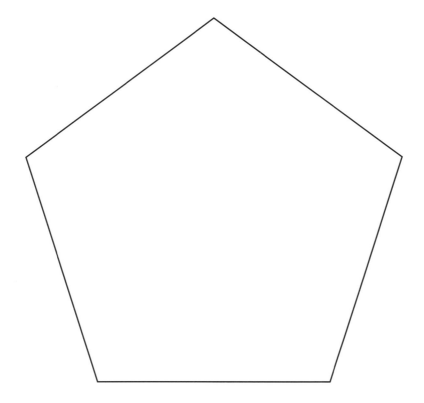

Its perimeter is 45 cm.

How long is each side?

Q 11
1 mark

---

12 Look at these symbols:

< > =

Write the correct symbol in the box.

5 × 10 [   ] 7 × 7

Q12
1 mark

Total

13 Jas completed a survey of children in her school. She wanted to know how many girls and how many boys there were of each age.

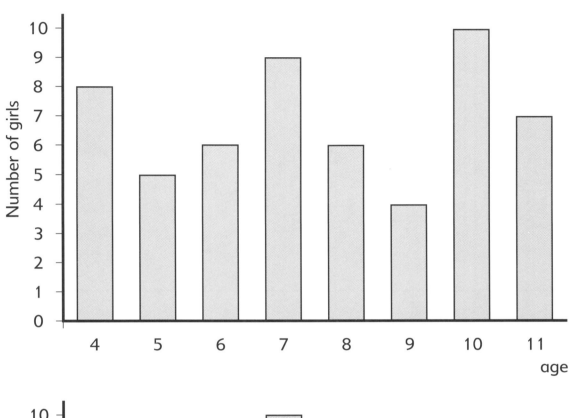

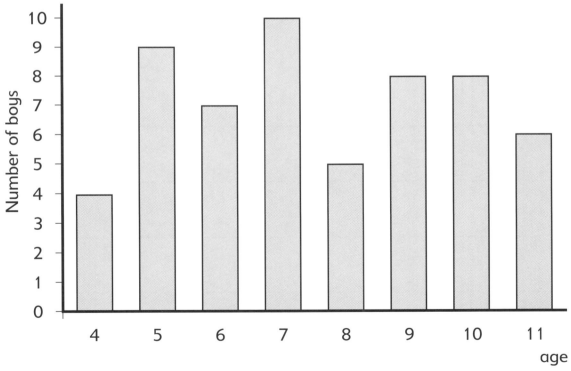

How many children were older than 9?

Q13
1 mark

Total

14 The teacher has £50 to spend on books for the class.

She chooses some books to the value of £37.60.

How much money has she got left to spend?

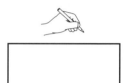

Q14
1 mark

15 Explain the rule for this sequence.

42   53   64   75   86

_____

_____

_____

_____

_____

Q15
1 mark

Total

16 The three numbers on each line add up to 1000.

Write the missing numbers.

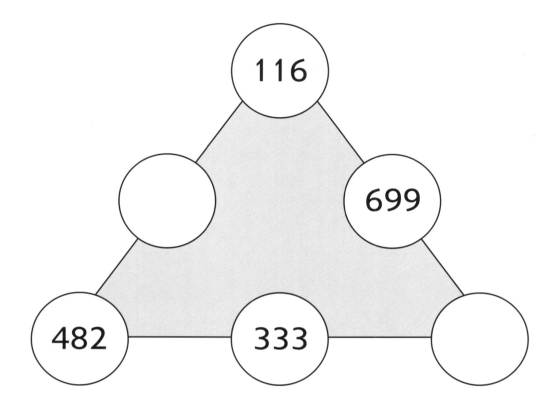

Q16
1 mark

Total

Test B2

17 Draw extra lines to complete the picture of a hexagon.

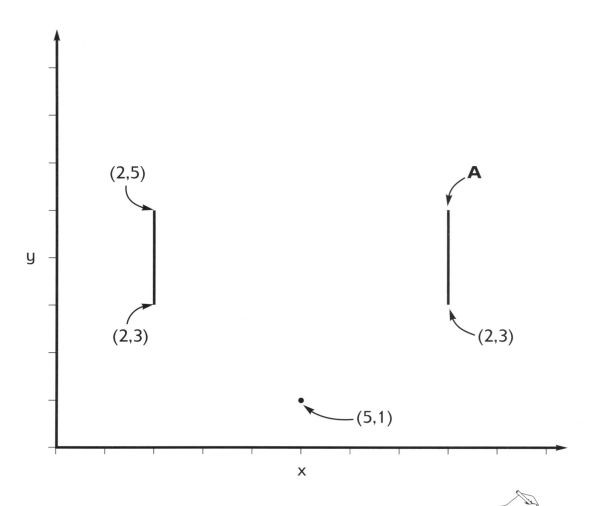

Give the co-ordinates of the point marked **A**.

Q17i
1 mark

Q17ii
1 mark

---

18 Calculate

$$\frac{1}{7} \text{ of } 343$$

Q18
1 mark

Total

19 The chart shows the times of some programmes on ABTV.

17.00 – 17.15	Newstime
17.15 – 17.50	Animal Antics
17.50 – 18.50	Football Fame
18.50 – 19.30	On the Beach
19.30 – 19.45	Focal Point

Which programme is on at 7 pm?

 _____

Q19i
1 mark

Which programme is on for the longest period of time?

 _____

Q19ii
1 mark

Total

20 Find all the pairs of factors for 24.

The first two have been done for you.

$$24$$

$$2 \quad \times \quad 12 \quad = 24$$

$$12 \quad \times \quad 2 \quad = 24$$

☞ [   ] × [   ] = 24

☞ [   ] × [   ] = 24

☞ [   ] × [   ] = 24

☞ [   ] × [   ] = 24

☞ [   ] × [   ] = 24

☞ [   ] × [   ] = 24

Q20
1 mark

Total

21 Complete each two-digit number to make it a multiple of 7.

| | 8 |

| 4 | |

| | 3 |

Q21
1 mark

Total

Answers to Test B2 (calculator)

When marking the children's work it is suggested that you enter marks in the boxes provided in the margins:

Enter 1 for a correct answer.

Enter 0 for an incorrect answer.

Enter – for no answer written.

Question	Answer	Mark	Notes
1	$\frac{4}{10}$ $\frac{2}{5}$	1	
2	625	1	
3	17, 19, 23	1	
4	4 x (12 – 2) = 40	1	
5		1	
6	183°	1	
7		1	
8	14766	1	Pupils may choose to work this out in writing or by using the calculator – ensure that they are accurate.
9	168 hours	1	

10i		1	Ensure hour hand is appropriately positioned between 11 and 12.
10ii	11.25 or 23.25	1	Pupils will not know whether the time is morning or evening so either answer is acceptable.
11	9cm	1	
12	>	1	
13	31	1	Note that the question says older than 9 and therefore 9 year-olds are not included.
14	£12.40	1	Ensure that pupils write £12.40 not £12.4.
15	Explanation should show that pupils understand that the sequence is going up in elevens.	1	
16	402, 185	1	
17i		1	Note that the hexagon can be completed correctly in more than one way.
17ii	(8, 5)	1	
18	49	1	
19i	On the Beach	1	
19ii	Football Fame	1	
20	8 x 3 3 x 8 6 x 4 4 x 6 24 x 1 1 x 24	1	
21	28, 42 or 49, 63	1	

Class record sheet

Names

Question																		
1																		
2																		
3																		
4																		
5																		
6																		
7																		
8																		
9																		
10																		
11																		
12																		
13																		
14																		
15																		
16																		
17																		
18																		
19																		
20																		
21																		
22																		
23																		
24																		
25																		
26																		